How Now Shall We Live?
STUDY GUIDE

HOW NOW SHALL WE LIVE?

STUDY GUIDE

CHARLES COLSON

AND NANCY PEARCEY

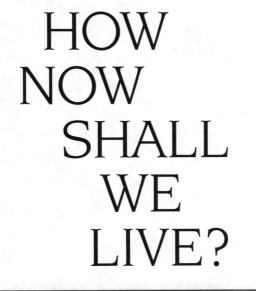

Tyndale House Publishers, Inc.
Wheaton, Illinois

Designed by Cathy Bergstrom

Edited by Lynn Vanderzalm

ISBN 0-8423-3607-9

Printed in the United States of America

05   04   03   02   01   00   99
8   7   6   5   4   3

CONTENTS

HOW TO GET THE MOST
OUT OF THIS BOOK

The lessons that follow are designed to guide you through a detailed and practical study of *How Now Shall We Live?* which we think you will find to be a provocative and informative, disturbing and hopeful, challenging and inspiring book. It is a call to arms for the members of the Christian community to break free of the intellectual and spiritual constraints that have pushed the church to the margin of society. The goal of this book is to equip us to begin the work of renewing and restoring the culture.

Session 1—the first thirteen lessons—covers the three worldview questions:

- Where did we come from, and who are we?
- What has gone wrong with the world?
- What can we do to fix it?

It explores the Christian worldview and demonstrates its superiority to the opposing worldviews of naturalism, Darwinism, moral relativism, multiculturalism, pragmatism, utopianism, existentialism, and post-modernism.

Session 2—the second set of thirteen lessons—addresses the follow-up question: How now shall we live? It challenges us to take seriously our responsibility to engage the world and be God's redeeming force to influence the family, education, the neighborhood, work, law and politics, science, the arts, and popular culture.

WHAT YOU WILL FIND IN EACH LESSON

With the exception of the last lesson, all the lessons follow the same format. The section marked Observe is designed to lead you in your reading of the assigned parts of *How Now Shall We Live?* Read through the questions *before* you begin reading the book because they will guide you in knowing what to look for in the chapters.

The section headed Reflect will take you through a study of one or more Scripture passages that will help you to think biblically about the subject, and to ensure that your growing Christian worldview is firmly established on the foundation of God's Word.

The section marked Apply will help you to think about what the ideas in the chapters mean for your life. Here you will have an opportunity to be honest about your own needs for Christian growth and to chart paths for a more powerful experience of the gospel of Jesus Christ.

The final section, marked Notes/Questions, gives you space to record notes about the chapter, insights or observations you may have, or unanswered questions you would like to share with a group.

The final lesson in Session 2 is designed to help you review what you have learned in this study and to establish a comprehensive plan for personal growth and ministry.

WHO CAN USE THIS GUIDE

We have designed this guide with enough flexibility to be used by either individuals or groups. Some people will want to use these lessons for their personal study of the book, and the write-in space will become a journal of their observations, responses, and goals.

Others will study the book with a group, whether that be a church group, a book group, or a group of neighbors. In such a setting, the study guide provides questions not only for personal preparation but also for group discussion and response.

We encourage you to study this book with a group, which will provide a forum for discussion, a springboard for action, and a tool for accountability. We don't expect you to agree with everything we say in *How Now Shall We Live?* But we do anticipate that the book will provoke lively discussion about a variety of themes and issues. We hope that your group wrestles with ideas presented in the book. We also hope that you come to a deeper understanding of your worldview. But most of all we hope that you are moved to act, to map out goals and strategies for becoming God's redeeming force in a new millennium.

As we said in the introduction to *How Now Shall We Live?*, the book is merely a beginning point for you to pursue what it means to live out a Christian worldview. Take a serious look at the list of resources in the recommended reading section at the end of the book. Choose several titles to deepen your understanding of specific topics that interest you. Our prayer is that God will bless this project and use it to bring profound renewal and revival in his church and our world.

SESSION ONE

1

CHRISTIANITY IS
A WORLDVIEW

Christianity is a *worldview*, that is, a way of understanding every aspect of the world and human life. For many of you, this is a new way of thinking about faith in Jesus Christ. But it is the *biblical* way, and once you grasp and begin to make use of it, a worldview understanding of Christianity will bring new excitement, enthusiasm, and power to your relationship with Jesus Christ.

Read the introduction and chapters 1 and 2.

OBSERVE

1 According to the introduction, how has failing to see Christianity as a worldview crippled Christians? _____

_____

_____

_____

_____

2 What is the difference between saving grace and common grace?_____

_____

_____

_____

3 What is the purpose of *How Now Shall We Live?*_____

_____

_____

_____

_____

4 Summarizing from chapter 1, make a list of the differences between the Detainees Pavilion of the García Moreno Prison and the wing that had been given over to the Prison Fellowship (PF) leaders:

Conditions in the Detainees Pavilion   Conditions in the PF Wing

_____   _____

_____   _____

_____   _____

5 To what may we attribute these differences? _____

_____

_____

6 In what ways is the García Moreno Prison a parable of God's kingdom at work in the midst of a fallen world? _____

_____

_____

_____

7 According to chapter 2, what is a *worldview?* _____

_____

_____

_____

8 What are the three questions that form the grid through which all worldviews can be evaluated? _____

_____

_____

_____

9 What is the basis for the Christian worldview? _____

_____

_____

_____

10 What is the "false dichotomy" that plagues much of contemporary evangeli-calism? _____

_____

_____

_____

11 What are the great commission and the cultural commission? How do we "engage the world"? _____

_____

_____

REFLECT

12 The Bible uses many contrasts to show that the Christian life is very different from life in the world. For example, Ephesians 2:1-5 speaks of the contrast between being dead in sins and being alive in Christ. What other contrasts can you find in Scripture? _____

_____

_____

_____

13 Read Ephesians 4:17-24, a classic passage comparing life in sin with life in Christ. How does Paul describe the effects of sin on those who still live in it (vv. 17-19)? _____

_____

14 Verse 20 is pivotal. What event in our lives cuts us off from the life of sin and sets us on a new course? Have you come to experience this? _____

_____

_____

15 What differences should new life in Christ make in our lives (vv. 21-24)?

_____

_____

16 What is the role of the mind in helping us to begin realizing this new life in Christ (compare vv. 17-19 with vv. 22-24)? _____

_____

_____

17 In what ways would people who have been "made new in the attitude of [their] minds" look at life differently from people who are "darkened in their understanding"? _____

_____

_____

APPLY

18 What new insights have you gained from these first two chapters? _____

_____

_____

_____

_____

19 How do you hope that reading this book will enrich or enhance your relationship with Christ? _____

_____

_____

_____

_____

20 In what areas of your life do you see your worldview having an impact? To help you respond to this question, make a list of the places you go and the kinds of activities you are involved with during a typical week. Be comprehensive and specific. Place a C next to the involvements that you can honestly say are shaped by a Christian worldview. _____

_____

_____

_____

_____

_____

_____

_____

_____

_____

_____

_____

_____

_____

21 Which of these areas still need to be influenced by a Christian worldview? Place an X next to each item that could use more "renewing of your mind" (Rom. 12:2).

22 How can your life begin to change as a result of renewing your mind according to a Christian worldview in these areas and activities?_____

_____

_____

_____

23 What prayer requests come to mind as a result of studying these chapters?

_____

_____

_____

_____

NOTES/QUESTIONS:

2

THE BATTLE OF THE AGE

The spiritual warfare in which we as Christians are constantly engaged is often played out on the stage of relationships and history, where our view of life comes into conflict with the views of those who are still darkened by their sin. To be prepared to do effective battle we need to understand the nature and scope of this worldview conflict.

Read chapters 3 and 4.

OBSERVE

1   According to chapter 3, what is naturalism? How is it opposed to theism?

_____

_____

2   What is relativism, and why is it a component in a naturalistic worldview?

_____

_____

3   What is pragmatism? _____

_____

_____

4   What is utopianism? _____

_____

_____

5   In what sense are we living in a *post*-Christian world? _____

_____

_____

6 How are existentialism and postmodernism related to multiculturalism?

_____

_____

7 How are these ideas opposed to the Christian worldview? _____

_____

_____

8 According to chapter 4, what is pre-evangelism? _____

_____

_____

9 What is apologetics? _____

_____

_____

10 What is the role of the mind in the life of discipleship? What is the state of the "Christian mind" today? _____

_____

_____

11 What is the mission of the church? _____

_____

_____

REFLECT

12 Perhaps nowhere in Scripture is the clash of worldviews more powerfully observed than in the story of the temptation of Christ in Matthew 4:1-11. Read these verses carefully. Who are the opponents here, and what is at stake in the outcome? _____

_____

_____

_____

13 In what ways do Satan's temptations appeal to pragmatism? to relativism?

_____

_____

_____

14 How is Satan tempting Christ to "live for the moment" (existentialism)?

_____

_____

_____

_____

15 In each case, how does Christ protect himself against Satan's wiles and frustrate the Tempter? _____

_____

_____

_____

_____

16 How can you see Christ's mind at work correcting Satan's false thinking and asserting a biblical worldview? _____

_____

_____

_____

_____

APPLY

17 In which of the areas and activities that you listed in the first lesson do you find that you are confronted by such things as naturalism, relativism, multiculturalism, pragmatism, utopianism, existentialism, and postmodernism? Give some examples. _____

_____

_____

_____

_____

_____

_____

18 Do you feel tempted to go along with these ways of thinking when they confront you? What makes that temptation so strong? _____

_____

_____

_____

19 How can these ways of thinking actually be Satan's instruments in the spiritual warfare? What is his purpose as he confronts us with these ideas? _____

_____

_____

_____

20 How can you prepare yourself to be victorious in the Lord in the face of such temptations? _____

_____

_____

_____

21 How can you use the tools of pre-evangelism, apologetics, and discipleship to strengthen your ability to have a positive influence on your world?_____

_____

_____

_____

_____

22 In what ways are you fulfilling the great commission? In what ways are you fulfilling the cultural commission? _____

_____

_____

_____

23 How does your personal "mission statement" line up with the mission of the church as expressed in this chapter? _____

_____

_____

_____

24 What prayer requests come to mind as a result of studying these chapters?

_____

_____

_____

_____

_____

NOTES/QUESTIONS:

3

THE RELIGION OF
NATURALISM—PART I

The modern world owes much to science and technology. Every day our lives are enriched and made easier by the discoveries, inventions, and products that have been developed by thousands of brilliant and well-meaning men and women. As long as science and technology function within proper limits, they are one of God's great blessings. But when they exceed their limits and reach into areas typically left for such disciplines as theology, philosophy, and ethics, then real problems can ensue—as Dave Mulholland discovered.

Read chapters 5–7.

OBSERVE

1 In chapter 5 we find Dave Mulholland on a trip to Disney World with his daughter, Katy. This trip was an eye-opener for Dave in three ways. What shocking realization did he make about each of the following?

- The place of God in the scientific worldview: _____

_____

_____

- Katy's view of religion in relation to science: _____

_____

_____

- Dave's ability to talk with his daughter about the biblical perspectives of what they heard and saw: _____

_____

_____

2 According to chapter 6, in what ways is the dominant view in our culture today "radically one-dimensional"? _____

_____

_____

3 Is naturalistic science neutral and objective? Why not? _____

_____

_____

4 How does naturalistic science, like religion, begin with certain faith assumptions? _____

_____

_____

5 In what ways did Carl Sagan's *Cosmos* attempt to provide a substitute for the Christian religion? _____

_____

_____

6 In what ways are Americans today being encouraged to believe in science as a religion? _____

_____

_____

7 According to chapter 7, what is big bang theory, and how can Christians use it to encourage belief in God? _____

_____

_____

_____

8 What is the anthropic principle, and how does it help you to express your confidence in God's creation of the world? _____

_____

_____

9 How does the world as it presently exists strongly suggest that it was designed by the Creator? _____

_____

_____

10 Take a look at 2 Peter 3:3-9. It's almost as if the apostle Peter could see ahead to our day and to the challenge that would be raised by naturalistic science. Those mocking believers' faith in Christ in Peter's day were *uniformitarian* in their view of the natural world. They said, "All things continue as they always have, so where's your God?" How is this like Dave's experience? _____

_____

_____

_____

11 In verse 4 Peter warns that mockers will deny God's promises by appealing to the stable course of nature. In what ways is this like the philosophy of naturalism? _____

_____

_____

_____

12 According to verses 5-6, what do these mockers deliberately ignore in order to make their argument? _____

_____

_____

_____

13 How does Peter account for the fact that the promise of the Lord's return has not yet been realized (vv. 7-9)? Why is he tarrying?_____

_____

_____

_____

14 What does this suggest about why we are here during this time when the gospel is being mocked and marginalized by the religion of science?

_____

_____

_____

15 Read 2 Corinthians 10:3-5. How are we to fight the battle with false philosophies, such as naturalism? _____

_____

_____

APPLY

16 In what ways have you observed that modern science claims to be the only genuine form of knowledge?_____

_____

_____

_____

17 How would you engage a proponent of naturalism in a discussion? How would you articulate your worldview?_____

_____

_____

_____

_____

18 What prayer requests come to mind as a result of studying these chapters?

_____

_____

_____

_____

NOTES/QUESTIONS:

4

THE RELIGION OF
NATURALISM—PART II

The more carefully we look at contemporary science, the more it confirms what the Bible teaches about life and the world.

Read chapters 8–10.

OBSERVE

1 According to chapter 8, how do scientists' attempts to create life in a test tube demonstrate that life is not a product of chance interactions of molecules?

_____

_____

2 How does the discovery of DNA support the idea of design and creation?

_____

_____

3 What is information theory? How does it affect the argument for design?

_____

_____

4 What is complexity theory? Does it establish a naturalistic account of life's origin? _____

_____

_____

5 According to chapter 9, what is Darwinism? _____

_____

_____

_____

6 How have studies in animal breeding actually served to discredit Darwinism instead? _____

_____

_____

_____

7 How do studies in genetic mutations discredit Darwinian thinking? _____

_____

_____

_____

_____

8 How does the concept of irreducible complexity discredit Darwinism? _____

_____

_____

_____

_____

9 In the face of so much contradictory evidence, why do naturalistic scientists continue to hold on to Darwinism? _____

_____

_____

_____

_____

10 According to chapter 10, why is Darwinism a dangerous idea? What "non-scientific" areas of life does it threaten to subvert? _____

_____

_____

_____

_____

11 On what does the authority of science rest today? How has Richard Lewontin helped to expose this false wizard? _____

_____

_____

_____

_____

12 Summarize the four points in the case for creation and design:

_____

_____

_____

_____

_____

_____

_____

_____

REFLECT

13 The best way of combating the religion of naturalism is by defeating it on its own turf, then bringing the gospel and the Word of God into the void that has been created. This is a biblical strategy, which can be seen by observing how the apostle Paul addressed some citizens of Athens. Read Acts 17:16-34. According to verses 32-34, what three reactions did listeners have to Paul's message in Athens? _____

_____

_____

14 What does Paul do in verses 16-18? What verbs describe his manner of speech among the Athenians? _____

_____

_____

15 On Mars Hill, did Paul begin with the Bible or something else (vv. 22-23)? What does he propose to do for the Athenians (see the last part of v. 23)?

_____

_____

16 Briefly trace the steps Paul took to get from his observation about their gods (v. 22) to the proclamation of coming judgment and the resurrection of Christ (v. 31): _____

_____

_____

_____

_____

APPLY

17 What steps can you begin to take to defend your children and the young people of your church against the false teachings of Darwinism and naturalism? _____

_____

_____

_____

_____

18 What kinds of results can you expect if you will take this challenge seriously? And if you don't? _____

_____

_____

_____

_____

_____

_____

19 Whose help will you enlist in doing this? _____

_____

_____

20 How can you engage the naturalistic scientists whom you know?

_____

_____

_____

_____

_____

21 What approach and reasoned arguments will you use? _____

_____

_____

_____

_____

22 What prayer requests come to mind as a result of studying these chapters?

_____

_____

_____

_____

NOTES/QUESTIONS:

5

LIFE WORTH LIVING

Socrates once said, "The unexamined life is not worth living."
We may go a step further and say that life is worth living only
when it is seen in the light of God's mercy and grace. And, from
that perspective, *every* life is worth living.

Read chapters 11–14.

OBSERVE

1 According to chapter 11, in what ways did God show his mercy and grace
   to Ken McGarity? _____

   _____

   _____

   _____

2 How did Ken finally come to realize that mercy and grace? _____

   _____

   _____

   _____

3 According to chapter 12, what are the main differences between the Christian
   and the naturalistic views of human life? _____

   _____

   _____

   _____

   _____

   _____

4 In what ways might we say that ours has become a "culture of death"? How did we become this way? _____

_____

_____

_____

_____

5 What is meant by "a radical dualism between body and soul," and why is this a problem? _____

_____

_____

_____

_____

6 What do we mean when we say, "Abortion has always been about more than abortion"? _____

_____

_____

_____

_____

7 What's wrong with the "choice" argument? _____

_____

_____

_____

8 According to chapter 13, in what ways does the Christian worldview provide a basis for the dignity of human life? _____

_____

_____

_____

9 How does the Christian worldview provide meaning and purpose for life?

_____

_____

_____

_____

10 How does the Christian worldview provide hope for the future? _____

_____

_____

_____

11 How does the Christian worldview motivate us to serve others?_____

_____

_____

_____

12 How does the story of Max (chapter 14) help us to see that every life is worth living when it is recognized as having been made in the image of God? _____

_____

_____

_____

REFLECT

13 The first chapters of Genesis give an account of the creation of human life. Let's take a look at Genesis 1:26-28, along with Genesis 2, where the details of Genesis 1:26-28 are elaborated. First, describe the significance for us, the bearers of the image of God, that God himself is

- spiritual: _____

_____

- rational:_____

_____

- moral: _____

_____

- social: _____

_____

- aesthetic ("good"):_____

_____

- creative:_____

_____

- active: _____

_____

14 From these passages, what mandates did God give human beings? How would our first parents have understood what God expected of them? _____

_____

_____

_____

_____

15 How did the mandates that God gave to Adam and Eve require them to use every aspect of their image-bearing potential? Refer to each of the attributes of that image outlined in question 13. Look back over the list of attributes that reflect God's image in us. How is each of these necessary for fulfilling the mandates that God has given to us? How are you using these different attributes in fulfilling these mandates? _____

_____

_____

_____

_____

_____

_____

APPLY

16 In which of the seven aspects of God's image do you believe you need to grow? Explain:_____

_____

_____

_____

_____

17 How would growing in these areas prepare you to be more effective in fulfilling the great commission and the cultural commission? _____

_____

_____

_____

_____

_____

18 What are the primary obstacles in the way of your acting more fully as one of God's image-bearers? What will you do to start overcoming these obstacles?

_____

_____

_____

_____

_____

_____

19 In what ways do you think your community would benefit if all the Christians in it lived fully as God's image-bearers? _____

_____

_____

_____

_____

20 Having studied the first worldview question—Where did we come from, and who are we?—what difference does it make to you that God created you in his image and has called you to carry out his work in the world? _____

_____

_____

_____

_____

_____

21 Having studied chapters 1–14, in what ways are you better equipped to articulate and defend your worldview?_____

_____

_____

_____

_____

22 What prayer requests come to mind as a result of studying these chapters?

_____

_____

_____

_____

_____

NOTES/QUESTIONS:

6

BUT FOR SIN

Have you ever heard someone say, "This would be a great place if it weren't for the people"? We could say the same thing, with far greater truth, about sin: This world and its people, societies, and cultures, would be a great place if it weren't for sin.

Read chapters 15–18.

OBSERVE

1 According to chapter 15, what has been the effect on humanity of Adam and Eve's first sin? _____

_____

_____

_____

2 What do Enlightenment thinkers propose as the cause of the human dilemma? What are some examples of this? _____

_____

_____

_____

_____

3 According to chapter 16, how can you see, even very early in Meg's experience with Synanon, that this would be a place where the lowest human inclinations would be encouraged? _____

_____

_____

_____

4 How do Charles Dederich's comments to Meg and Jack during their first meeting reveal that he and Synanon held to an Enlightenment view regarding the cause of the human dilemma?_____

_____

_____

_____

5 In what ways did Synanon become like a religion for Meg? _____

_____

_____

_____

_____

6 According to chapter 17, what is meant by a "utopian vision of a new age"?

_____

_____

_____

7 Briefly summarize how the idea of sin came to be discarded in Western societies. What was the role of such ideas as freedom, Marxism, and fascism in this process? _____

_____

_____

_____

8 According to chapter 18, in what ways are many Americans today caught up in the myth of utopianism? _____

_____

_____

_____

9 How does the utopian myth appear in each of the following?

• psychology:_____

_____

• education: _____

_____

• law: _____

_____

- welfare: _____

_____

- criminal justice:_____

_____

10 How does the denial of sin ultimately make us vulnerable to the schemes of social planners? _____

_____

_____

REFLECT

11 Let's take a closer look at sin's first appearance and some of its effects. Read Genesis 3:1-6. How does sin arise as rebellion against God and his word?

_____

_____

_____

12 By what particular avenues did sin make itself appealing to Eve (v. 6)?_____

_____

_____

_____

13 According to verse 7, what was the first consequence that Adam and Eve experienced after their sinful choice? (Compare with Gen. 2:25.)_____

_____

_____

_____

14 What effects of sin are evident in each of the following verses from Genesis 3?

- v. 8: _____

_____

- v. 12: _____

_____

- v. 16: _____

_____

_____

- vv. 17-19: _____

_____

_____

_____

APPLY

15 Where do you see the influence of the utopian worldview in your life?_____

_____

_____

_____

16 How is this worldview encouraged by the following?

- advertising: _____

_____

- consumerism: _____

_____

- news media: _____

_____

17 How can our understanding of the reality of sin prepare us to overcome the temptations of utopian thinking? _____

_____

_____

18 Will people you know be receptive to the idea that sin lies at the root of the human dilemma? Why or why not? _____

_____

_____

_____

19 What prayer requests come to mind as a result of studying these chapters?

_____

_____

_____

_____

_____

NOTES/QUESTIONS:

7

THE NATURE OF SIN

Sin has wrought havoc throughout God's creation. We are all tempted and tainted by sin. None of us escapes its powerful effects. But what *is* sin?

Read chapters 19 and 20.

OBSERVE

1 According to chapter 19, what does this statement mean: "The face of evil is frighteningly ordinary"? _____

_____

_____

_____

2 How do people who hold a naturalistic worldview try to account for evil?

_____

_____

_____

3 What have been some of the factors leading people to set aside the idea of sin?

_____

_____

_____

_____

4 What is the popular culture's attitude toward sin today? _____

_____

_____

_____

5 How is the utopian mind-set related to the rejection of sin? _____

_____

_____

_____

6 What is the "fatal flaw in the myth of human goodness"? _____

_____

_____

7 How does society try to hold sin in check? To what degree is it unable to do this? _____

_____

_____

_____

_____

8 According to chapter 20, what is involved in obeying God? _____

_____

_____

_____

9 How does the Bible account for the entrance of sin and evil into the world?

_____

_____

_____

10 What do nonbelievers need to see?_____

_____

_____

_____

REFLECT

11 Let's take a further look at the biblical doctrine of sin. Read Romans 5:12-21. How did sin come into the world and reach into our lives? _____

_____

_____

_____

12 Look carefully at Romans 3:10-18. According to Paul, how does sin affect each of the following? Cite the relevant verses in your answer.

- our moral life: _____

_____

_____

- our understanding of things: _____

_____

_____

- our speech and conversation: _____

_____

_____

- our relationships with other people:_____

_____

_____

- our relationship with God: _____

_____

_____

13 How does God's law help us to understand sin (see Rom. 3:19-20 and Rom. 7:7)?_____

_____

_____

_____

14 How does society's rejection of God's law influence the presence of sin in our culture? _____

_____

_____

_____

15 According to Romans 6:11-19, what does the Christian worldview prescribe as the proper attitude toward sin?_____

_____

_____

_____

_____

16 As individual followers of Christ, where must we begin in the battle to roll back sin (Rom. 6:23)? What does this require of you (Rom. 6:11-19)? _____

_____

_____

_____

_____

17 What are some ways that we can help one another in this important and difficult challenge? _____

_____

_____

_____

_____

_____

18 What are some ways Christians can begin to speak out against sinful practices in our communities? What kinds of responses can we expect when we do?

_____

_____

_____

_____

19 Since only the gospel can deliver people from the power of sin, how can we effectively bring the gospel message to those around us? _____

_____

_____

_____

_____

20 What prayer requests come to mind as a result of studying these chapters?

_____

_____

_____

_____

_____

NOTES/QUESTIONS:

8

THE PROBLEM OF SUFFERING

Innocent children murdered in their classrooms and schoolyards. Refugees driven ruthlessly from their homes. Abused spouses and children. Good people suddenly struck down by illness or accident. Why does God allow so much suffering in the world?

Read chapter 21.

OBSERVE

1 What problem was bothering Albert Einstein? Why was it on his mind at this particular time? How did this problem affect his view of God?_____

_____

_____

_____

_____

_____

2 What did Einstein conclude about the problem of suffering? How did this affect his response to God? _____

_____

_____

_____

_____

3 How have atheists tried to solve the problem of evil and suffering? _____

_____

_____

_____

_____

4 How have Eastern religions and Christian Science tried to solve this problem?

_____

_____

_____

_____

5 How have some theologians tried to solve this problem?_____

_____

_____

_____

6 How has "process theology" tried to solve the problem of suffering?_____

_____

_____

_____

7 How has John Hick tried to solve it? _____

_____

_____

_____

8 Why is it so important that we recognize the historicity of the Fall in the Garden?_____

_____

_____

_____

_____

9 Why is it necessary for God to condemn evil? _____

_____

_____

_____

10 How did God in his mercy respond to evil and suffering in his creation? _____

_____

_____

_____

11 How should people respond to God's mercy in the face of evil? _____

_____

_____

_____

_____

REFLECT

12 Revelation 12 can give us some additional insights into the origins of evil and suffering on earth. According to verses 7-9 and verse 13, how did evil come to be on the earth? _____

_____

_____

_____

13 A passage that complements this one very well and that biblical scholars understand to treat the same subject is Ezekiel 28:1-19. While the king of Tyre is the immediate object of the prophecy, the story of Satan's condemnation lies in the background (as can be seen from vv. 2, 12-15). According to verses 2, 15, and 17, what attitude in Satan brought about his downfall?

_____

_____

_____

_____

14 According to Revelation 12:9 and 13, what did Satan take as his "mission" once he was on the earth? How could this lead to evil and suffering? _____

_____

_____

_____

_____

15 According to Revelation 12:17, who are the special objects of Satan's rage? Why do you suppose this is so? _____

_____

_____

_____

_____

APPLY

16 Whenever we are confronted with evil and suffering—whether in our own lives or in our society—how should we respond? _____

_____

_____

_____

17 What should we keep in mind about the ultimate source of suffering? _____

_____

_____

_____

18 What should our attitude be toward those who suffer? _____

_____

_____

_____

19 What does it mean for those of us who worship and serve God that he in his mercy has taken steps to relieve human suffering? _____

_____

_____

_____

_____

20 Think of a recent incident in which people in your community were subjected to suffering—through crime, accident, storm, or similar circumstances. How might your church have responded in order to show God's love? _____

_____

_____

_____

_____

21 What steps can your church take today in order to be ready for the next opportunity to show God's love to those who are suffering? _____

_____

_____

_____

_____

22 Having studied the second worldview question—What has gone wrong with the world?—what difference does it make to you that we live in a fallen world marked by sin?_____

_____

_____

_____

_____

_____

23 Having studied chapters 15–21, in what ways are you more equipped to articulate and defend your worldview?_____

_____

_____

_____

_____

24 What prayer requests come to mind as a result of studying this chapter?

_____

_____

_____

_____

NOTES/QUESTIONS:

9

FROM DEATH
TO LIFE

Our culture has been described as "a culture of death" because it glorifies violence, tolerates abortion, and flirts with euthanasia. But as many people who helped to create this culture of death are finding out—people like Dr. Bernard Nathanson—God still offers us a new life.

Read chapters 22 and 23.

OBSERVE

1 According to chapter 22, briefly summarize the process that Dr. Nathanson went through as his mind began to change about abortion. What were some of the factors involved? _____

_____

_____

_____

_____

2 What did Dr. Nathanson discover from watching ultrasound images of abortion? _____

_____

_____

_____

3 How did proponents of abortion respond to Dr. Nathanson's change of heart? Why? _____

_____

_____

_____

4 What in Dr. Nathanson's upbringing led him to regard abortion as perfectly natural and normal? _____
_____
_____

5 What happened to cause Dr. Nathanson's heart to begin to turn to God?
_____
_____

6 According to chapter 23, what is "the great human predicament," and how does Bernard Nathanson's experience illustrate it? _____
_____
_____
_____

7 What kind of redemption is promised through the medium of advertising?
_____
_____
_____

8 Discuss some of the ways that this promised redemption is presented. How do these ads try to appeal to religious hopes? _____
_____
_____
_____

9 Why is materialism no true redemption at all? What does it fail to provide?
_____
_____
_____

REFLECT

10 Scripture says a lot about the false gods that people construct to take the place of the one true God. Read Romans 1:18-20. Which aspect of chapters 22 and 23 does this passage address? _____
_____
_____
_____

11 What do we learn from verses 21-23 about people's inherent religious inclinations? What do many people do with the knowledge they have of God?

_____

_____

_____

12 If we think of a "god" as anything to which we give ultimate devotion, anything in which we stake our hope of happiness, what would be some examples of false gods today? _____

_____

_____

_____

13 According to verses 24, 26, and 28, how does God respond to people when they reject him in favor of false gods? _____

_____

14 Look carefully at verses 24-32. How would you describe the moral trend that sets in when people reject knowledge of the true God and begin to pursue false gods? Where do you see that happening in our society today? _____

_____

_____

_____

_____

APPLY

15 Do you think it's possible for Christians to keep false gods? How? Do you recognize any false gods in your own life? If so, what will you do about it?

_____

_____

_____

16 What would you recommend for any Christian who is seeking to serve the false gods of our materialistic age? _____

_____

_____

_____

17 According to Romans 1:21, how can we keep from falling into the materialistic religion of our age? _____

_____

_____

_____

18 Why do many young people get caught up in the allure of materialism? How can parents and churches help children recognize and resist this false god?

_____

_____

_____

_____

_____

19 How does the gospel of Jesus Christ give greater satisfaction and hope than the empty promises of materialism? _____

_____

_____

_____

20 What prayer requests come to mind as a result of studying these chapters?

_____

_____

_____

_____

NOTES/QUESTIONS:

10

LIBERATED
TO SLAVERY

"Although they claimed to be wise, they became fools," Romans 1:22 tells us. This might well be a banner displayed over our postmodernist generation. Many people believe that by throwing off the restraints of religion and morality, they will attain true liberation. However, instead of finding freedom, they find that they have become slaves to base lust and unquenchable desire.

Read chapters 24 and 25.

OBSERVE

1 According to chapter 24, what is the "the myth of progress" or "the Escalator Myth"? What does it promise? _____

_____

_____

2 How is the Escalator Myth related to the ideas of sin, utopia, and evolution?

_____

_____

_____

3 What did Hegel contribute to the Escalator Myth? _____

_____

_____

4 In what ways is Marxism a form of the Escalator Myth?_____

_____

_____

_____

5 In what ways do the ideas of Karl Marx reflect a religious worldview? _____

_____

_____

_____

6 What is the fatal flaw of Marxism? _____

_____

_____

_____

7 According to chapter 25, who was Margaret Sanger, and what was her contribution to the Escalator Myth? _____

_____

_____

_____

8 How did Alfred Kinsey try to detach sex from morality? What justification did he offer? _____

_____

_____

_____

9 How did Wilhelm Reich help to accelerate this version of the Escalator Myth? _____

_____

_____

_____

10 In what ways can we see—especially in the work of Robert Rimmer—that this version of the Escalator Myth is another form of religion promising redemption? _____

_____

_____

_____

11 How is sex education shaped by the Escalator Myth? _____

_____

_____

_____

12 In what ways do the founders of this worldview demonstrate the emptiness of their views in their own lives?

REFLECT

13 The desire to be free of God's law is very old. Look at Psalm 2:1-3. In what ways does this picture capture the "liberationist" hopes that we see all around us today?

14 According to verses 4-6, how does God respond to people's liberationist aspirations?

15 In verses 6-9, what does God proclaim as the divine counterpart of human liberation thinking?

16 What should be our response to God's divine authority?

APPLY

17 How should Christians respond to the vain aspirations of our "liberated" contemporaries?

18 Are you prepared to do that with the people around you? In what ways would you like to be better prepared? _____

_____

_____

_____

19 How would you put Psalm 2:10-12 into a meaningful presentation of the good news of God's love in Jesus Christ? _____

_____

_____

_____

20 What prayer requests come to mind as a result of studying these chapters?

_____

_____

_____

_____

NOTES/QUESTIONS:

11

SALVATION THROUGH SCIENCE

 M any people today still put their faith in science and technology to make a better world, even though the scientific version of the Escalator Myth is increasingly called into question in our post-modernist culture.

Read chapter 26.

OBSERVE

1 How does popular culture portray the hope of redemption through science and technology? _____

_____

_____

_____

_____

2 How did Francis Bacon start the ball rolling in this version of the Escalator Myth? _____

_____

_____

3 How did Auguste Comte envision the role of science in the development of a mature society?_____

_____

_____

4 What was Herbert Spencer's contribution to the myth of progress and the religion of science? _____

_____

_____

_____

5 How have genetic studies factored into this version of the Escalator Myth?

_____

_____

_____

_____

6 Why is science unable to give any moral guidance? _____

_____

_____

_____

_____

7 What danger for human dignity lies in this version of the Escalator Myth?

_____

_____

_____

_____

_____

8 How has this kind of thinking influenced extraterrestrial studies? In what ways can you see a religious element to this field? _____

_____

_____

_____

_____

9 Does history support the idea that science—or knowledge—is a reliable savior? Explain: _____

_____

_____

_____

_____

10 How should we understand the role of science within a biblical worldview?

_____

_____

_____

REFLECT

11 Genesis 11:1-9 shows us a primitive society with lofty ideals and high hopes. According to verses 1-4, to what did these people aspire? How would those goals be expressed in contemporary language? _____

_____

_____

_____

_____

_____

12 How are these goals at odds with God's will?_____

_____

_____

_____

_____

13 What danger did God see in this project? How did he defeat it? _____

_____

_____

_____

14 It is interesting to note that God sometimes works gently in his judgments against rebellious people. Here, instead of wrath and destruction, he used a simple cultural artifact—language—to thwart the arrogant plans of his creatures. What does this reveal to us about God's love toward those who rebel against him? What should we learn from this for our own relationships with people who live in opposition to God? _____

_____

_____

_____

_____

15 In the end, would you say that humanity even benefited from this act of judgment? In what ways? _____

_____

_____

_____

APPLY

16 What evidence do you see to indicate that many people are still looking for science to take us along the road to utopia? _____

_____

_____

_____

_____

17 In what kinds of settings in our communities might we expect to find proponents of the scientific worldview promoting their version of the Escalator Myth? How can we begin to oppose them there? _____

_____

_____

_____

18 In evaluating current technology, many people in the scientific community believe that "If we *can* do it, we should." What kinds of moral questions does such thinking provoke? How can a biblical worldview help in addressing those questions? _____

_____

_____

_____

_____

19 What prayer requests come to mind as a result of studying this chapter?

_____

_____

_____

_____

NOTES/QUESTIONS:

12

THE COURAGE
OF DESPAIR

The failure of so many modern ideologies led many people to despair of really changing human nature or creating a better world. With Western worldviews crumbling, some people turn to the East.

Read chapters 27 and 28.

OBSERVE

1 According to chapter 27, what caused people to begin to doubt the promise of science and technology? _____

_____

_____

2 What is existentialism? _____

_____

_____

3 In what ways did existential thinking appeal to the countercultural movement of the sixties? _____

_____

_____

_____

4 How did the various strains of pessimism dovetail nicely into the predominant Darwinian views of the day? _____

_____

_____

_____

5   What is sociobiology, and how does it express a philosophy of despair?

_____

_____

_____

_____

6   According to chapter 28, why did some people begin looking to Eastern religions for redemption? _____

_____

_____

_____

_____

7   How did the popular culture help to spread the gospel of Eastern religion and the New Age? _____

_____

_____

_____

_____

8   What is the New Age movement? How does it differ from traditional Eastern thinking? _____

_____

_____

_____

_____

9   How has New Age thinking affected many people's view of God? _____

_____

_____

_____

10   By what means is New Age thinking making its way into our society?

_____

_____

_____

_____

11 Why is the New Age god unable to save us? _____

_____

_____

_____

_____

_____

REFLECT

12 In John 4:1-27 we read that Jesus confronted a woman who was confused
about religion—among other things. How did Jesus go out of his way—
in more ways than one—to talk with this woman (vv. 4, 9)? _____

_____

_____

_____

_____

13 How did Jesus approach this woman (v. 7)? _____

_____

_____

_____

_____

14 How did he turn a mundane conversation into a spiritual discussion
(vv. 10-15)? _____

_____

_____

_____

15 What did Jesus do to show this woman that religion and morality are inextri-
cably linked (vv. 16-18)? _____

_____

_____

16 How did Jesus get this woman to see him for who he is (vv. 19-26)? _____

_____

_____

_____

APPLY

17 What can we learn from Jesus' encounter with the Samaritan woman about helping people with different religious views to begin thinking about Jesus and the claims of the gospel? _____

_____

_____

_____

_____

18 Think of one person with whom you might begin to use what you have learned, starting this week. How will you approach him or her to get the conversation started? _____

_____

_____

_____

_____

19 What prayer requests come to mind as a result of studying these chapters?

_____

_____

_____

_____

NOTES/QUESTIONS:

13

REAL REDEMPTION

Only in the gospel of Jesus Christ can people find real redemption. Christ takes us the way we are—fallen and sinful—and accepts our repentance and forgives our sin. He paid the ultimate price for our sin with his own death on the cross. Now he offers us power for both meaningful living today and everlasting life beyond the grave. That's real redemption!

Read chapter 29.

OBSERVE

1 Briefly summarize the promise of redemption as each of the following offers it:

• commercialism:_____

_____

_____

• neo-Marxism:_____

_____

_____

• sexual liberation:_____

_____

_____

• science and technology:_____

_____

_____

• the New Age:_____

_____

_____

2 What is the human dilemma according to the Christian worldview? Explain:

_____

_____

_____

_____

3 What does Christianity present as the solution to this problem? _____

_____

_____

_____

_____

_____

4 Why is it important to stress that Christianity's solution is rooted in historical truth?_____

_____

_____

_____

_____

5 In what ways does the Old Testament point to the Christian solution?

_____

_____

_____

_____

6 What does it mean that God's redemption _restores_ us?_____

_____

_____

_____

_____

7 How does this restoration get us back on track with God and his plan?

_____

_____

_____

_____

8 Let's take a look at Hebrews 2:1-9. What warning does the writer give us (vv. 1-3a)? _____

_____

_____

_____

9 In verses 5-8 the writer describes the purpose for which God created us—the purpose to which we are restored in redemption. He quotes from Psalm 8. What purpose for humanity is outlined in Hebrews 2:6-8a? _____

_____

_____

_____

_____

10 In what ways can we see that this pupose has not yet been fulfilled—that people are not succeeding in subduing the creation for God's glory and human benefit? _____

_____

_____

_____

11 Verse 9 begins with the word *but*, and the writer points us to the solution. What is it? What can begin to get us back on track with God's plan for humanity? _____

_____

_____

_____

APPLY

12 How did you come to know Christ and the restoring grace of God? What difference has that made in your life? _____

_____

_____

_____

_____

_____

13 In what areas of your life can you say that you are consciously and consistently taking a "Psalm 8" approach to living for the Lord, that is, seeking to bring all things in line with God's purpose for creation? _____

_____

_____

_____

_____

14 In what areas of your life do you need to develop this approach more fully?

_____

_____

_____

_____

_____

15 What is implied in the writer's question—"How shall we escape?" (Heb. 2:3)—if we fail to take seriously the full implications of our redemption in Christ?_____

_____

_____

_____

_____

16 What is required for us to "pay more careful attention" (Heb. 2:1) to the things we have heard about redemption in Jesus Christ? _____

_____

_____

_____

17 Having studied the third worldview question—What can we do to fix it?— what difference does it make to you that God redeemed you through the death of his Son and promises you eternal life with him? _____

_____

_____

_____

_____

_____

_____

18 Having studied chapters 22–29, in what ways are you more equipped to articulate and defend your worldview?_____

_____

_____

_____

_____

19 As we reach the halfway point in our study, what have been some of the most important lessons you have learned so far? _____

_____

_____

_____

_____

_____

20 What prayer requests come to mind as a result of studying this chapter?

_____

_____

_____

_____

NOTES/QUESTIONS:

SESSION

TWO

1

ALL THINGS NEW

The gospel of Jesus Christ is the power of God for salvation, a salvation that makes all things new in our lives, as Danny Croce and untold millions of men and women throughout the ages have discovered.

Read chapters 30 and 31.

OBSERVE

1 Referring to chapter 30, summarize the steps that led Danny Croce to a saving knowledge of the Lord Jesus Christ. _____

_____

_____

_____

2 What evidence can you see that Danny truly came to know the Lord?_____

_____

_____

_____

3 According to chapter 31, what is the status of the cultural commission (or cultural mandate) today? _____

_____

_____

4 What is the relationship between the cultural commission and the great commission? Explain: _____

_____

_____

_____

5 What does it mean that Christians are saved not only *from* something but also *to* something? _____

_____

_____

_____

_____

6 Why should there be no dichotomy between the "sacred" and the "secular" for the Christian? _____

_____

_____

_____

7 In what ways did the Irish Christian missionaries of the fifth to the eighth centuries—beginning with Patrick, the British missionary to the Irish— effectively combine the cultural commission with the great commission?

_____

_____

_____

_____

8 In what other ways did Christianity serve as a creative cultural force during the Middle Ages? _____

_____

_____

_____

_____

9 Why is today an excellent time for Christians to begin once again to live and proclaim their faith boldly?_____

_____

_____

_____

10 What is the key to effective evangelism? Explain: _____

_____

_____

_____

_____

REFLECT

11 Read 2 Corinthians 5:14-21. According to the apostle Paul, what must be our compelling motivation as we go forth in the name of Jesus? Explain: _____

_____

_____

12 What does Christ's example teach us (v. 15)?_____

_____

13 Verse 17 says that anyone who is in Christ is a new creation. List the areas in your life in which that newness is increasingly evident: _____

_____

_____

_____

_____

_____

_____

_____

14 Paul says we have been given a "ministry of reconciliation." What does that mean? How does the idea that God is reconciling the world (the entire world order) to himself challenge the false dichotomy between the "sacred" and "secular"? _____

_____

_____

_____

15 As ambassadors for Christ, how should we expect to conduct our lives in this postmodernist world? _____

_____

_____

_____

APPLY

16 Go back to question 13 above. On a scale of 1 to 10 (10 meaning "fully" and 1 meaning "not at all"), to what extent would you say that you are experiencing

the newness of Christ in each of these areas of your life? Give an explanation for each of the areas that you rate less than 6: _____

_____

_____

_____

_____

17 Since Christian unity is an important part of our witness for Christ, how can you begin to encourage more unity among the members of your congregation? between your congregation and other churches in your community?_____

_____

_____

_____

_____

18 What is the message that we—as Christ's ambassadors—have to proclaim to our postmodernist world?_____

_____

_____

_____

19 What prayer requests come to mind as a result of studying these chapters?

_____

_____

_____

_____

NOTES/QUESTIONS:

2

BEGINNING WITH OURSELVES

The place to begin in realizing more of the newness of Christ and the power of a Christian worldview is with ourselves. We all need to overcome old habits and unprofitable ways of thinking.

Read chapter 32.

OBSERVE

1 Referring to the example given early in the chapter, how is it apparent that the secular worldview affects the thinking even of sincere Christians? _____

_____

_____

2 What has become of the sense of individual responsibility in our post-modernist world? _____

_____

_____

3 What is a "value-free lifestyle"? In what ways is this concept evident in our day? _____

_____

_____

_____

4 What is the "modernist impasse"? Why does this make today an opportune time for Christians to share their worldview?_____

_____

_____

_____

5 In what ways do social statistics encourage us to believe that we have a powerful message to proclaim? _____

_____

_____

_____

6 How should the example of a scholar like Guenter Lewy encourage us in our work as reconcilers and ambassadors?_____

_____

_____

_____

7 In what ways has it been shown that having a sincere religious faith can be beneficial to one's health? _____

_____

_____

_____

8 In what ways do the results of research in the world of psychology encourage us in our witness? _____

_____

_____

_____

9 Summarize the ways in which the Christian worldview provides help and hope for our postmodernist generation. _____

_____

_____

_____

_____

REFLECT

10 The early Christians lived in ways that gave powerful confirmation of their witness to Jesus Christ. According to Acts 2:41-47, what was the congregational life of the first Christians like? _____

_____

_____

_____

11 Read Acts 4:32-37. How does this add to the picture of the first Christian community?_____

_____

_____

12 In what ways and for what purposes was the life-changing power of the gospel at work in Acts 6:1-6?_____

_____

_____

_____

13 Read Acts 6:7. These priests had no doubt seen and heard Jesus, and they had heard others tell about Jesus. How might the events of Acts 6:1-6, in addition to those of Acts 2 and 4, have influenced these priests to believe in Jesus? Explain:_____

_____

_____

_____

14 Think about the churches in our own communities. When the postmodernist world looks at us, to what extent does it see reflected in our lifestyles and relationships the kinds of things those priests would have seen in the first Christian church? What can we learn from those first Christians? _____

_____

_____

_____

_____

APPLY

15 What attitudes does it take for Christians to begin relating to one another and to the world around them as the first Christians did? In which of these attitudes does your church need to grow? In which do you need to grow?

_____

_____

_____

_____

16 Can you see any ways—either in your own life or that of your church—in which the ideas of secularism have affected your approach to the Christian life? _____

_____

_____

_____

_____

17 From what we saw in those first Christians, what is required for us to overcome our captivity to secular thinking and to gain the new worldview and attitudes that will cause the watching world to take notice? _____

_____

_____

_____

_____

18 What can you begin to do today to realize more of the power of the Christian worldview in your own life? _____

_____

_____

19 What obstacles might keep you from making progress in this effort? How can your fellow church members help you to overcome these? _____

_____

_____

_____

_____

20 What prayer requests come to mind as a result of studying this chapter?

_____

_____

_____

_____

NOTES/QUESTIONS:

3

GOD'S TRAINING GROUND

In recent years the idea of "family" has been subjected to drastic redefinition by our postmodernist society. A biblical worldview can help us to recover the true meaning and purpose of this foundational social unit.

Read chapter 33.

OBSERVE

1 In what ways is the family today being redefined? From what sources?_____

_____

_____

_____

_____

2 Why is it important that we ask people not only to explain but to *justify* their worldview? What does this mean? _____

_____

_____

_____

_____

_____

3 Why is it so important to root the idea of marriage and family in God's creation? _____

_____

_____

_____

_____

4 How does the philosophy of the "unencumbered self" affect the family and other social institutions? _____

_____

_____

_____

5 What has social science revealed about the ability of many divorced people to serve as effective parents? to function as happy and fulfilled adults? _____

_____

_____

_____

_____

6 Outline the essential teachings of a biblical view of the family:_____

_____

_____

_____

_____

7 What does it mean for Christians to treat their own families as a ministry?

_____

_____

_____

8 What are some things that local churches can do to begin promoting healthier families among their members and in their community? _____

_____

_____

_____

_____

_____

9 What are "Community Marriage Policies," and how do they help communities to strengthen families? _____

_____

_____

_____

_____

REFLECT

10 Read Ephesians 5:18–6:4, a passage that has much to say about how families ought to operate. According to verse 18b, what is the source of healthy family life? Why is this so? _____

_____

_____

_____

11 One of the evidences of our actually being filled with God's Spirit is that we submit to one another. What does this mean? How did Jesus embody this practice for us in John 13:1-15? _____

_____

_____

_____

12 What does it mean for a wife to submit to her husband? for a husband to submit to his wife? _____

_____

_____

_____

_____

13 What should a husband take as the measure and standard of his love for his wife? Give some examples of what this might look like. _____

_____

_____

_____

14 Look carefully at Ephesians 5:25-33. How will a husband show that he truly loves his wife as Christ loved the church? How will a wife show that she is willing to submit to that love?_____

_____

_____

_____

_____

15 According to Ephesians 6:1-4, what are the responsibilities of Christian parents toward their children? of children toward their parents? _____

_____

_____

_____

_____

APPLY

16 What is the most important lesson that you have gained from this study? How can you begin to implement this lesson in your own family life? _____

_____

_____

_____

_____

_____

17 How can Christian families help one another to realize more of the biblical promise for families? _____

_____

_____

_____

_____

18 As you begin to work harder at realizing the promise of Scripture for your family, what will be your greatest obstacles? How will you overcome these? Whose help will you enlist? _____

_____

_____

_____

_____

_____

19 What prayer requests come to mind as a result of studying this chapter?

_____

_____

_____

_____

4

STILL AT RISK

It is hardly necessary to talk about the sad state of many of America's schools. Their problems are in no small part a result of the naturalistic worldview that dominates the educational arena. What can Christians do about it?

Read chapter 34.

OBSERVE

1   What are the two historic tasks of American education, and how well are American schools addressing these tasks today?_____

_____

_____

_____

2   How has an emphasis on self-esteem affected the learning process in our schools? _____

_____

_____

_____

3   What is a "constructivist" view of education, and how does it differ from traditional theories of education? _____

_____

_____

_____

_____

4 What view of the child prevails in America's schools? How does that view work against effective learning? _____

_____

_____

_____

5 What faulty assumptions about children guide this view of learning? _____

_____

_____

_____

6 How does the American education system view the idea of redemption and the role of the school in the redemptive process? _____

_____

_____

_____

7 What is the starting point of a biblical view of education, and how is it unique? _

_____

_____

8 What options are available for the education of Christian children today? What do you consider to be some of the strengths and weaknesses of these various options? _____

_____

_____

_____

_____

9 What are some approaches that Christians might take to begin improving the public schools in their communities? _____

_____

_____

_____

_____

10 Why is it so important that Christians begin to be active in the work of school reform and the education of children in our communities? _____

_____

_____

_____

REFLECT

11 Psalm 78:1-8 provides excellent guidelines for the education of our children. According to verses 3-4, who is responsible for the education of children?

_____

12 According to verse 4, what must we teach our children about God? What is our responsibility to ensure that all academic disciplines are taught from the perspective of a biblical worldview? _____

_____

_____

_____

_____

_____

13 One area of the curriculum for our children is mentioned in verse 5. What is it, and what does it include? _____

_____

_____

_____

14 According to verses 6-7, what should be the long-term objectives of our work in educating our children? _____

_____

_____

_____

_____

15 According to verse 8, what are we trying to prevent? _____

_____

_____

APPLY

16 To what extent and in what ways is it possible for parents in your community to take an active role in the education of the community's children?_____

_____

_____

_____

17 How are you or any of your church members involved in any of these?

_____

_____

_____

18 What can we expect if Christians remain detached from the work of educating children? _____

_____

_____

19 How can your church begin to take a more active role in seeing to it that its own children receive an education that is consistent with the biblical worldview? _____

_____

_____

_____

20 What prayer requests come to mind as a result of studying this chapter?

_____

_____

_____

_____

NOTES/QUESTIONS:

5

LIFE TOGETHER

Our communities are in trouble. They are under assault from the dark side of the naturalistic worldview, and they seem wholly unable to defend themselves and to preserve a sense of cohesiveness, safety, and well-being. The biblical worldview points us toward solutions to this desperate situation.

Read chapters 35 and 36.

OBSERVE

1 According to chapter 35, what made Sal think that he could make a difference in his community? _____

_____

_____

_____

2 How would you describe Sal's approach to trying to make a difference in his community? _____

_____

_____

_____

_____

3 What evidence indicates that Sal actually did help his community begin to change? _____

_____

_____

_____

_____

4 According to chapter 36, how did the Supreme Court exacerbate the problems of crime in the neighborhoods of America? _____

_____

_____

_____

_____

5 In what ways does the worldview behind the civil liberties movement reject biblical teaching? _____

_____

_____

_____

_____

6 How do American cities try to combat the effects of the civil liberties movement? _____

_____

_____

_____

_____

7 What does *shalom* mean, and how does it relate to the idea of community? In what ways have Christians begun to show that *shalom* is a workable idea in communities? _____

_____

_____

_____

_____

_____

8 In what ways do the examples from Boston, Dallas, Chicago, Baltimore, and other cities mirror the work done by Sal Bartolomeo in his neighborhood?

_____

_____

_____

_____

9 How does our citizenship in the City of God require us to take responsibility for the *shalom* of our communities? _____

_____

_____

_____

REFLECT

10 Christians can be a powerful force for community, beginning in their own congregations. Read Acts 6:1-6, and summarize the problem that arose there:

_____

_____

_____

11 In what ways was this an *economic* problem? In what ways was it a *racial* problem? _____

_____

_____

_____

12 What steps did the individual church members take to resolve this situation? What steps did the leaders of the community take?_____

_____

_____

_____

13 According to verse 7, what resulted from this direct effort at restoring *shalom* in the Christian community? _____

_____

_____

APPLY

14 What problems are threatening or depriving your community of its *shalom* today? _____

_____

_____

_____

15 How is your community trying to cope with these problems? Are they getting better or worse? _____

_____

_____

_____

_____

16 How will you get involved in restoring *shalom* to your community? How will your church get involved? _____

_____

_____

_____

_____

17 What can we expect if Christians fail to get involved? What can we expect if they do become involved? _____

_____

_____

_____

_____

18 What prayer requests come to mind as a result of studying these chapters?

_____

_____

_____

_____

NOTES/QUESTIONS:

6

BECOMING MORAL PERSONS

Christians have shown that communities can be restored to *shalom* by working one person at a time, one situation at a time. But what does it mean to become a "moral person"?

Read chapter 37.

OBSERVE

1   Why doesn't relativism provide a foundation for a safe and orderly society?

_____

_____

_____

_____

2   How does the example of the Conference on Science, Philosophy, and Religion demonstrate the inability of reason alone to create a moral consensus for society? _____

_____

_____

_____

_____

_____

3   What role should conscience play in achieving a moral society? How does this notion relate to the biblical worldview? _____

_____

_____

_____

_____

4 How has our sense of separation between public life and private life affected the morality of Americans? How does the Christian worldview respond to this false dichotomy? _____

_____

_____

_____

_____

5 What is integrity, and why is it so important? _____

_____

_____

_____

6 How does the biblical worldview help people achieve integrity? _____

_____

_____

_____

7 What did I (Chuck) fail to understand as a young lawyer about individual morality? How did it catch up with me? _____

_____

_____

_____

8 How can we begin to fulfill the moral law of God? _____

_____

_____

_____

9 If only converted people can fulfill the law of God, why do Christians have a responsibility to work for a good society "by cultivating ethical knowledge even among the unconverted"? _____

_____

_____

_____

10 Through what positive and negative means do societies encourage virtuous behavior? What is the state of these means in our society today? _____

_____

_____

_____

_____

_____

REFLECT

11 Read Psalm 51. David experienced moral failure in his sin against Bathsheba and against her husband. But according to David, against whom did he really sin (v. 4)? How did he characterize his behavior? _____

_____

_____

12 David expresses his feelings of guilt, sorrow, and repentance in this psalm. Are these negative responses? What useful purposes do they serve? How do we see these responses in our society today? _____

_____

_____

_____

_____

13 David expresses two goals in this psalm. The first can be seen in verses 12-13. What is it? _____

_____

_____

14 The second is expressed in verses 18-19. What is it? _____

_____

_____

15 How can individual reconciliation with God be a blessing not only to the individual but also to his or her community? _____

_____

_____

_____

_____

16 According to verse 17, where does moral transformation begin? What is the relationship between the gospel of Jesus Christ and what we read in this verse?

_____

_____

_____

APPLY

17 Can we expect the members of our community to become moral people apart from being converted to Christ? Will keeping the law of God save them?

_____

_____

_____

_____

18 What does this mean for your work as a moral agent in your community? Are you prepared to take up this challenge? _____

_____

_____

_____

19 How can you and your church demonstrate faithfulness to biblical morality to the members of your community? _____

_____

_____

_____

_____

20 What prayer requests come to mind as a result of studying this chapter?

_____

_____

_____

_____

NOTES/QUESTIONS:

7

THE WORK OF
OUR HANDS

The Protestant work ethic has long undergirded the American economy, making it one of the strongest and most productive in the world. But even a work ethic grounded in Scripture can be corrupted by a naturalistic worldview. It's time to reestablish a Christian presence in the workplaces of America.

Read chapter 38.

OBSERVE

1   How can we see that God intended work to be part of his plan for a world filled with *shalom?* _____

_____

_____

2   How did the fall into sin affect the work that people were given to do? _____

_____

_____

3   How are Christians to view wealth? _____

_____

_____

4   What does it mean that we are only stewards of the things God has entrusted to us? How does this relate to our work? _____

_____

_____

_____

_____

5 What is the Bible's view of private property? _____

_____

_____

_____

6 In the biblical worldview, what becomes of the poor? _____

_____

_____

_____

_____

7 How did Enlightenment views begin to corrupt the biblical view of work?

_____

_____

_____

8 On what factors does a healthy economy depend? What does this mean?

_____

_____

_____

_____

_____

9 In what ways has the workplace begun to work against healthy community life? _____

_____

_____

_____

10 How are churches today providing models of programs that can spur economic self-sufficiency?_____

_____

_____

_____

_____

_____

REFLECT

11 Let's look more closely at the biblical basis of work as we see it described in Genesis 2. Looking at verse 2, what is the basis for saying that God created people as working creatures? _____

_____

_____

_____

_____

12 Notice how many times Genesis 1 uses the words *good* or *very good* to describe God's work. What does it mean that God described his work as good? What does this suggest about God's intentions for our work? _____

_____

_____

_____

_____

_____

_____

_____

13 Various kinds of work are indicated or suggested in Genesis 2. What kinds of work do the following verses lead you to think about?

▪ v. 9: _____

_____

▪ v. 10: _____

_____

▪ vv. 11-12: _____

_____

▪ v. 15: _____

_____

▪ vv. 19-20: _____

_____

▪ vv. 22-24: _____

_____

_____

14 How was the calling to work related to the cultural mandate of Genesis 1:26-28? _____

_____

_____

_____

APPLY

15 To what extent and in what specific ways is your own work consciously related to your calling as an image-bearer of God? Looked at another way, how does your work allow you to labor for the realization of God's "good" in your community? _____

_____

_____

_____

16 Do you see any signs of the deterioration of the Christian work ethic in your community? Explain: _____

_____

_____

_____

17 What can your church do to begin preparing its young people to enter the workforce with a biblical view of work as their operating framework?

_____

_____

_____

18 In what ways can you or your church begin to reclaim the workplace in your community for a more biblical view of work? _____

_____

_____

_____

19 What prayer requests come to mind as a result of studying this chapter?

_____

_____

_____

_____

NOTES/QUESTIONS:

8

THE ULTIMATE APPEAL

The Christian apologist Francis Schaeffer used to talk about the dangers of "sociological law"—laws written to respond only to particular social situations, having no basis in anything other than the needs of the moment. But, without a foundation in absolute law, sociological law can become tyrannical, as we shall see.

Read chapter 39.

OBSERVE

1 On what basis did Dr. Martin Luther King Jr. decide to disobey the law in Birmingham? Do you agree with King's reasoning? his actions? _____

_____

_____

_____

_____

2 What is the difference between just and unjust law? _____

_____

_____

_____

_____

3 What does it mean that there exists "transcendent law above human law"?

_____

_____

_____

_____

_____

4 In what ways does the American system of government and law as designed by the Founders reflect biblical principles? _____

_____

_____

_____

5 What is the meaning of "sphere sovereignty"? How does this concept contribute to the idea of limited government? _____

_____

_____

_____

_____

6 What have been the effects of pragmatism and deconstructionism on transcendent law? _____

_____

_____

_____

7 How did the Supreme Court redefine "liberty" in *Planned Parenthood v. Casey*? What are the implications of this redefinition? _____

_____

_____

_____

_____

_____

8 What did the Court label as "majoritarian intolerance"? In *Lee v. Weisman* what did the Court reject as "intolerance"? _____

_____

_____

_____

9 How does the Court's view of intolerance increase its own power? _____

_____

_____

_____

_____

10 What did the momentous Supreme Court ruling against the Religious Freedom Restoration Act (RFRA) signify? _____

_____

_____

_____

11 How do liberal and conservative approaches to the law and morality create a catch-22? _____

_____

_____

_____

_____

12 What is "the great vulnerability of the American system" of government?

_____

_____

_____

_____

13 List the four consequences of the loss of moral authority:

_____

_____

_____

_____

14 How are we already suffering from these consequences? To what extent do you find this frustrating? challenging? _____

_____

_____

_____

15 Given the rejection of moral law in society and the imbalance of power in the government, what seems to be the best way to restore our legal and political systems? _____

_____

_____

_____

_____

REFLECT

16 Psalm 72 is an excellent place to look at God's plan for human governments. How does this psalm guide us in praying for our governments, according to each of the following verses?

- v. 1: _____

_____

- v. 2: _____

_____

- v. 4: _____

_____

- v. 5: _____

_____

- vv. 12-14: _____

_____

- v. 15: _____

_____

17 What promises does God make to governments that rule according to his guidelines (see Ps. 72:3, 7, 8-11, 15-17)? _____

_____

_____

_____

18 Ultimately, according to verses 18-19, what happens in a community or society in which people are governed according to God's law? _____

_____

_____

19 Imagine that you are writing a letter to a candidate for political office listing guidelines you would expect him or her to use when making decisions in office. What would you write? _____

_____

_____

_____

_____
_____
_____
_____

APPLY

20 How frequently do you pray for your political leaders and government officials? How can this psalm help you in praying more effectively? _____
_____
_____
_____

21 How can we "live out our convictions as responsible citizens" and present the Christian worldview to our communities? _____
_____
_____
_____

22 Have you ever been labeled "intolerant" for your beliefs or for a stand you have taken? Describe the situation. _____
_____
_____
_____

23 What is our responsibility when we are confronted with an unjust law? _____
_____
_____
_____
_____

24 What prayer requests come to mind as a result of studying this chapter?
_____
_____
_____
_____
_____

NOTES/QUESTIONS:

9

THE BASIS FOR
TRUE SCIENCE

Within the Christian worldview science can be a powerful tool.
But first it must be stripped of its naturalistic assumptions and
retooled with the presuppositions of revealed truth.

Read chapter 40.

OBSERVE

1   In what ways is it apparent that science is used as a weapon against religious
    faith? _____
    _____
    _____
    _____

2   What was David Hume's role in helping to position science as an adversary
    to religion?_____
    _____
    _____

3   In what ways are the naturalistic assumptions of science incoherent and
    contradictory? _____
    _____
    _____
    _____

4   What task does the Christian community face in responding to these assump-
    tions?_____
    _____
    _____

5 What four important assumptions did the Christian worldview provide for the first scientists? _____

_____

_____

_____

_____

6 In what kinds of forums should Christians be trying to raise issues regarding the fallacies of naturalism in science? _____

_____

_____

_____

7 What goals can we set for addressing naturalistic science in the schools?

_____

_____

_____

_____

8 Why should we encourage Christian young people to go into the field of science as their work? _____

_____

_____

_____

_____

9 Many scientists today are pressing to reestablish the claims of science on a foundation of false religion. What are they failing to remember? _____

_____

_____

_____

10 What is meant by "the reformation of science"? _____

_____

_____

_____

_____

REFLECT

11 Let's look more closely at the passage with which chapter 40 concludes. Read 2 Corinthians 10:3-5. To what kind of people was Paul writing (see 1 Cor. 1:26)? Whom did he expect to see getting involved in the teaching of 2 Corinthians 10:3-5? _____

_____

_____

12 Paul says, "The weapons we fight with are not the weapons of the world." Why does he refer to our struggle with "arguments" and "pretension" as warfare? Have you experienced this warfare? In what ways? _____

_____

_____

_____

13 Paul tells us that God's weapons are quite powerful to accomplish the results we seek. According to Ephesians 6:10-18, what are those weapons? _____

_____

_____

_____

_____

14 Who or what are our adversaries in this warfare (2 Cor. 10:4-5)? How can we identify them in the world today? _____

_____

_____

_____

15 What is our twofold objective in this warfare (v. 5)? What would that look like, say, in the case of modern science? _____

_____

_____

_____

APPLY

16 In what ways have you seen the adverse affects of the naturalistic worldview on the practice of your own faith? Has the naturalistic outlook colored or otherwise hindered your faith in any way? Explain: _____

_____

_____

_____

_____

_____

_____

17 What do you think it would take for you to be ready to talk with someone else about the fallacies of naturalistic thinking? How can you become better prepared? _____

_____

_____

_____

_____

_____

18 How can your church become more involved in speaking out against the fallacies of the naturalistic worldview in the various forums available to you in your community? _____

_____

_____

_____

_____

_____

19 What can we expect if Christians fail to take up this challenge and naturalism continues its warfare against the faith without any opposition? _____

_____

_____

_____

_____

_____

20 What prayer requests come to mind as a result of studying this chapter?

_____

_____

_____

_____

NOTES/QUESTIONS:

10

REFORMING THE ARTS

The arts are a powerful tool for shaping opinion and touching the heart. Christians must engage the arts with their worldview so that music, art, and literature will glorify God and enrich the human experience.

Read chapters 41 and 42.

OBSERVE

1   How does the opening vignette of chapter 41 illustrate the power of the arts to affect our outlook on life? _____

_____

_____

_____

_____

2   How does the story of Henryk Górecki illustrate the power that a Christian worldview can have on the arts? _____

_____

_____

_____

_____

3   According to chapter 42, why are so many contemporary composers producing such dissonant music? Why are so many modern artists creating so much abstract art? _____

_____

_____

_____

_____

4 Why are the arts important to the Christian? _____
_____
_____

5 How do the arts function in society? What seems to be their purpose?
_____
_____
_____

6 Cite some historical examples of Christians working in the arts. How have
they used the arts to testify of their faith in Christ?_____
_____
_____
_____
_____
_____

7 What caused the arts to veer off the path marked out by so many exemplary
Christian artists? _____
_____
_____
_____
_____

8 In what sense has art today become a surrogate for religion?_____
_____
_____
_____

9 What is meant by the term *anti-art?* What are some examples?_____
_____
_____
_____

10 What steps can Christians take to begin restoring the arts? _____
_____
_____
_____

REFLECT

11 The Bible not only endorses the arts but also shows us that God uses them widely. Which of the arts does God employ in each of the following situations?

- building the tabernacle and the temple: _____

_____

- writing the psalms: _____

_____

- preparing the priestly garments: _____

_____

12 One passage in particular helps us to see God's approval and use of the arts in the reformation of society. Read Exodus 35:20–36:7. How did God intend to use the arts (vv. 20-21)? Which of the arts would be involved? _____

_____

_____

_____

_____

_____

_____

13 In what ways was art a community activity in this passage?_____

_____

_____

_____

_____

14 Where did Bezalel and Oholiab get their skills as artists? _____

_____

_____

15 Why do you suppose the Lord mentioned the particular gift he did in verse 34? What does this suggest about the importance of the arts for people in general? _____

_____

_____

16 How did the people show that they were eager to support the arts and the work of the artists who had been called to serve the Lord? _____

_____

_____

_____

APPLY

17 Think about your own home for a moment. In what ways do the arts play a role in the way you live and in what your home "says" to any visitors?

_____

_____

_____

18 How would you rate your ability to appreciate and benefit from the arts in general (good, fair, poor)? Do you think your love for God and other people could be enhanced by a more consistent involvement with the arts? Why or why not? _____

_____

_____

_____

_____

19 Where will you begin to help in restoring the arts to their God-honoring position in society? How will you become more aware of and active in the arts yourself? What can your church do to enrich its use of the arts? _____

_____

_____

_____

_____

_____

20 What prayer requests come to mind as a result of studying these chapters?

_____

_____

_____

NOTES/QUESTIONS:

11

THE GOSPEL AND
POPULAR CULTURE

Can even popular culture be redeemed and used for good within the framework of a biblical worldview? You might just be surprised.

Read chapters 43 and 44.

OBSERVE

1   According to chapter 43, how would you describe Martha Williamson's early experience as a Christian working in Hollywood? _____
_____
_____

2   Why was deciding to do *Angel's Attic* such a struggle for Martha? How was her faith at work in the midst of this struggle? _____
_____
_____
_____

3   How would you describe Martha's efforts to keep *Touched by an Angel* on the air? What can we learn from her about reforming popular culture? _____
_____
_____
_____

4   According to chapter 44, why is the challenge of redeeming popular culture so great? _____
_____
_____

5 What has happened to popular culture as it has spread and pervaded our society? _____

_____

_____

_____

6 In what ways can popular culture adversely affect people? _____

_____

_____

_____

7 What is a good working definition of *popular culture?* Using this definition, in what ways are you exposed to popular culture every day? _____

_____

_____

_____

_____

_____

8 What does it mean to begin linking "art to truth"? _____

_____

_____

9 How can Christians begin to redeem popular culture? _____

_____

_____

_____

_____

_____

_____

10 Should Christians be involved in creating popular culture? Why or why not?

_____

_____

_____

REFLECT

11 The Bible provides several examples for us to follow in working to redeem popular culture. First, however, we need to be convinced that this is legitimate. How do the following Scripture passages suggest that redeeming popular culture can be considered a legitimate and important work for Christians?

- 1 Cor. 3:21-23: _____

_____

- 1 Cor. 10:31: _____

_____

- Eph. 1:22-23: _____

_____

12 Look at the psalm dedications for such psalms as 55, 56, and 57. These psalms were apparently meant to be sung to popular songs or according to well-known tunes. How do they guide us in thinking about ways to redeem popular culture? What are some examples of how people do this today? _____

_____

_____

_____

_____

13 Jesus used literary art forms to communicate objective truth. How does his use of parables, metaphors, similes, and so forth serve to encourage us in the use of such forms? _____

_____

_____

_____

_____

14 The Bible itself, particularly the New Testament, uses popular culture in the form of language. The Greek used in the New Testament, for example, was the "language of the people" of its day, not of the academics or philosophers. How should this guide and encourage us in thinking about the potential of popular culture to serve the purposes of God? _____

_____

_____

_____

_____

APPLY

15 Think about the influence of popular culture in your own life. In what ways do the following affect your lifestyle?

- advertisements: _____

_____

- popular music: _____

_____

- television programs: _____

_____

- conversations with others: _____

_____

- the print media: _____

_____

16 Do you think that, on the whole, popular culture is a positive or negative factor in your walk with the Lord? Explain: _____

_____

_____

_____

_____

17 Where will you begin to redeem popular culture in your own life? in your home and family? _____

_____

_____

_____

18 What can churches do to prepare their young people to take their own popular culture "captive" for Jesus Christ? _____

_____

_____

_____

_____

19 How can your church encourage and support its members who become involved in creating popular culture? _____

_____

_____

_____

_____

20 What prayer requests come to mind as a result of studying these chapters?

_____

_____

_____

_____

NOTES/QUESTIONS:

12

HOW NOW SHALL
WE LIVE?

It is not enough to know that a Christian worldview is more consistent, more rational, and more workable than any other worldview. We need to find ways to let that worldview work for us if it is going to be as effective as God intends.

Read chapter 45.

OBSERVE

1 For what reasons is the Christian worldview to be preferred over all other worldviews? _____

_____

_____

_____

2 What is the real test of a worldview and of the Christian worldview in particular? _____

_____

_____

3 What events led Kim Phuc to become a follower of Christ? _____

_____

_____

_____

4 What was her immediate response to coming to know the Lord?_____

_____

_____

_____

5 How was Kim able to use her experience as a way of testifying to the grace of God in her life? _____

_____

_____

_____

6 How did Kim's message of forgiveness accomplish what Robert McNamara's technological worldview could not? In what ways is this an excellent parable of how we should now live? _____

_____

_____

_____

_____

_____

7 How, in a few brief sentences, would you answer the question, "How now shall we live?" _____

_____

_____

_____

_____

_____

_____

REFLECT

8 Ephesians 5:1-21 shows us the many contrasts and challenges involved in living the life of faith. According to verses 1-2, what will be the most obvious indicator that we are imitating God and walking as Christ did? _____

_____

_____

9 According to verses 3-8, what must we avoid in order to live consistently in the light of God's truth and love? _____

_____

_____

_____

_____

10 What should we be seeking to cultivate more of, according to verses 9-10?

_____

_____

11 What, according to verses 11-13, should be the effect of our living "in the light" on the unfruitful works of darkness? What does this mean? _____

_____

_____

_____

_____

12 Paul says we are to be careful about how we live (v. 15). Here is a call to vigilance in every area of our lives. What four things do verses 15-18 say we should we be vigilant about, and what will result from this vigilance? _____

_____

_____

_____

_____

13 If we fail to exercise this kind of vigilance over our lives, what can we expect in a time such as ours, when truly "the days are evil" (v. 16)? _____

_____

_____

_____

14 Paul calls us to be filled with (literally "in") the Spirit. If wine is to be taken both literally and as a symbol of the worldliness all around us, what kinds of things must not be allowed to fill up our lives? _____

_____

_____

_____

15 What four evidences of the Spirit's presence in a believer's life does Paul identify in verses 19-21? What would they look like in your life? _____

_____

_____

_____

_____

_____

APPLY

16 Evaluate your walk with the Lord by the criteria outlined in this passage. Would you say that you are fully consistent with this passage, somewhat consistent, somewhat inconsistent, or altogether inconsistent with what we see here? Explain: _____

_____

_____

_____

_____

17 How would you encourage new believers to begin exercising the kind of vigilance that Paul calls for in this passage? _____

_____

_____

_____

_____

_____

18 How can you discern when your life is too much filled with some aspect of worldliness? What should you do when this is the case? _____

_____

_____

_____

_____

19 How can Christians encourage one another to walk in the light as this passage calls us to do? _____

_____

_____

_____

_____

20 What prayer requests come to mind as a result of studying this chapter?

_____

_____

_____

_____

_____

NOTES/QUESTIONS:

13

BECOMING MEN AND WOMEN OF ANOTHER TYPE

This final lesson is designed to help you bring together your thoughts, observations, and conclusions from your study of *How Now Shall We Live?* By the time you complete this lesson, you will have developed a personal plan of action for moving ahead in the Christian worldview.

REVIEW

1 What new insights have you had from your study of this book? In what ways have those ideas begun to affect your approach to living as a Christian in this world? _____

_____

_____

_____

_____

_____

_____

2 In what ways has the worldview of naturalism had a greater effect in your life than you think it should? _____

_____

_____

_____

_____

3 In what ways have you begun to adopt a more consistently biblical worldview as the guiding framework for your life? _____

_____

_____

_____

_____

_____

4 In what new areas of study or growth have you been challenged by this book? What do you intend to do to keep growing in these areas? _____

_____

_____

_____

_____

_____

5 In what ways will you begin to be more effective in working for a restoration of biblical thinking in your community? _____

_____

_____

_____

_____

6 How can your church take a more active role in restoring biblical thinking in your community? How will you facilitate that? _____

_____

_____

_____

_____

PLAN FOR ACTION

7 It's a good idea to have a plan of action if we want to make the most of what we have learned from our study of *How Now Shall We Live?* Let's see what this might involve by examining one of the apostle Paul's ministry plans. Read

Romans 15:14-33. Paul has a long-range objective in mind here. According to verse 24, what is it? _____

_____

8 This objective comes right out of his own personal ministry vision, which he summarizes in verses 15-19. What was Paul's vision for ministry? _____

_____

_____

_____

_____

9 Paul also had several short-range objectives he wanted to accomplish. What are they, as you see them in the following verses?

- vv. 25-26: _____

_____

- v. 29: _____

_____

- v. 24: _____

_____

10 Paul's vision and objectives were accomplished by a ministry strategy. He planned to visit Jerusalem as well as the church in Rome and then live among the lost in Spain. What kinds of ministry did he intend to do in these places?

- v. 16: _____

_____

- vv. 18-19: _____

_____

- v. 20: _____

_____

- v. 24: _____

_____

- v. 26: _____

_____

- v. 31: _____

_____

11 While Paul was in Rome, he hoped to gather supplies—and probably team members—from the Roman believers for his trip to Spain. What spiritual rationale did Paul give for expecting the Romans to share in his ministry like this (v. 27)? _____

_____

_____

_____

APPLY

12 Paul's plan of action was based on these elements:

- a personal ministry vision
- long-range objectives
- short-range objectives
- a ministry strategy
- help from other believers

13 A personal plan of action for moving ahead in the Christian worldview begins with a personal ministry vision. What is your ministry vision? How do you define what God is calling you to fulfill as his agent in the world? _____

_____

_____

_____

_____

_____

14 A personal plan of action calls for some long-range objectives. What can you identify as your long-range objectives in seeking to be more consistent and effective in living the Christian worldview and working for the restoration of biblical thinking in your community and the world? _____

_____

_____

_____

_____

_____

15 Short-range objectives are the steps that will get us moving in the direction of achieving our long-range objectives. In each of the areas below, identify two or three short-range objectives for moving ahead.

- things I need to study: _____

_____

_____

_____

- areas I need to begin changing: _____

_____

_____

_____

- personal spiritual disciplines I need to develop: _____

_____

_____

_____

- people I need to start reaching out to: _____

_____

_____

_____

_____

- people I need to encourage to join me: _____

_____

_____

_____

- areas in which I can serve in my church: _____

_____

_____

_____

_____

16 Your ministry vision and objectives will be accomplished through a strategy in which you use your ministry gifts. What are the primary kinds of ministry that you intend to be involved in as you put into practice the Christian worldview? _____

_____

_____

_____

_____

17 Paul recognized that we can't fulfill our visions, goals, and ministries without help. He looked to the Romans to help him get to Spain. Who are the key people most likely to be able to help you? What do you need from each of them? _____

_____

_____

_____

_____

_____

18 Talk to the people you indicated above and share your personal ministry vision, objectives, and strategy with them. Are they willing to help you?

_____

_____

_____

_____

19 What other believers will you help as they try to live the Christian worldview? How will you help them (Heb. 10:24)? _____

_____

_____

_____

_____

20 Complete the following: "More than anything else, I hope and pray that my studies in *How Now Shall We Live?* will enable me to _____

_____

_____

_____

_____

21 What prayer requests come to mind as a result of studying the overview of *How Now Shall We Live?* _____

_____

_____

_____

_____

NOTES/QUESTIONS: